A GERMAN PRINTER

PETER BEDRICK BOOKS
New York

Contents

Introduction

This book tells the story of a boy called Martin who lived round about AD 1485. He and his family lived in the city of Nuremberg. Today, Nuremberg is in Germany, but in those days it was part of a great empire. This empire was called the Holy Roman Empire and it stretched across many countries in south eastern Europe.

Martin's father is a printer, who makes his living by printing playing cards, souvenir pictures and pictures of the saints. Many other craftsmen lived in Nuremberg; the city was famous throughout the Empire for its skilled goldsmiths, jewelers and metalworkers. At the time the story begins, Martin's father has just been given an important order to print books for a famous publishing firm.

In 1485 printed books were a new invention; before then they had been written slowly and painstakingly by hand. The Chinese had discovered how to print using moveable type (lots of individual letters arranged to make words, sentences and then whole pages of text) about 400 years before that, but no one in the West knew of their invention. About 30 years before this story begins, a German printer, called Johannes Gutenberg, had invented a way of printing very like the Chinese system. His invention was widely copied, and printing presses were set up throughout Europe. Thousands of printed books were quickly produced, and towns like Nuremberg became important centers of the printing trade.

This book also tells the story of Martin's friend, Albrecht, and is very closely based on fact. Albrecht grew up to be a very famous artist, Albrecht Dürer, and you can see his drawings, paintings and woodcuts in many of the famous art galleries around the world.

At the end of the book, you can see detailed pictures of the fine items the craftsmen produced in Nuremberg at this time.

The Last Day at School

The schoolmaster's voice droned on and on, but Martin didn't hear a word. He could hardly wait for the day's lessons to end. Then he would be free of school – for ever! He was 12 now, and his father had decided he should leave.

His last day at school had begun in the usual way. In the morning, the boys had taken part in the service in St Lorenz's church. Afterwards there had been the usual long Latin lessons. Martin hated Latin, even though the schoolmaster was always telling him how important it was.

'Most things worth studying are still written in Latin,' he would say. 'Our city of Nuremberg is famous for its men of learning. You must work hard to try and be like them.'

Martin didn't want to be a scholar. He was happy if he could do just enough schoolwork each day to get by without being caned. He gazed out of the window at the steep roofs and tall towers of the city. Soon he would be out there instead of in this stuffy room.

The schoolmaster's voice made him jump. 'We all know you're leaving soon, Martin,' the master said, 'but just try to pay attention while you're here. What did I say just now?'

Martin shook his head, and tried to think of something to say in reply.

The schoolmaster sighed and frowned. 'We are reading about the Emperor's treasures,' he said. 'Look, on this page the Latin tells us about his jewelled crown and sword, and his glittering armor. Of course,' the schoolmaster continued, 'the Emperor's greatest treasures are the Holy Relics. Do you know that they are nearly 1500 years old? Our city is very fortunate to have them in its keeping. Just imagine, there is a piece of the cross on which Jesus was put to death, and a splinter from the manger where he slept when he was a newborn baby! People come hundreds of miles to catch a glimpse of these Relics.

'Now, come on, Martin! Let's see if you can read the next sentence for us.'

Albrecht in Trouble

On his way home from school, Martin decided to call in to see his friend Albrecht, who had left school the previous year. Albrecht now worked as an apprentice to his father, who was a goldsmith. It would take him at least three years to learn the basic skills of the goldsmith's trade. Then he would be free to hire himself out to work for other master craftsmen as a journeyman, who was a laborer paid by the day.

The goldsmith's workshop was in the metalworking district of the city. Nuremberg was famous as a center where all sorts of metal objects were made. Master craftsmen, like Albrecht's father, were very skilful and grew rich and highly respected. As Martin walked along, he looked through the open windows of the workshops. Goldsmiths, silversmiths, needlemakers, nail and wire makers, cutlers, swordsmiths and armorers were all hard at work.

When Martin reached Albrecht's workshop, he was surprised to see Albrecht outside in the street, looking worried and upset.

'What's the matter?' Martin asked.

'I'm in trouble at home,' said Albrecht. 'My father is angry with me. I've just given him a shock. I have told him that I no longer want to be a goldsmith.'

Martin stared at his friend. Not want to be a goldsmith! The goldsmiths were the most famous of all Nuremberg craftsmen, and Albrecht's father had a particularly successful business. 'What do you want to do instead?' he asked.

'I want to be a painter,' said Albrecht.

Martin was amazed. 'A painter! I didn't know you wanted to be a painter! Whatever did your father say?' he gasped.

There was no time for Albrecht to reply.

'Come here, boy! At once!' His father's voice rang out loudly in the street. With a grimace, Albrecht turned and ran indoors.

9

Who is Master Koberger?

As he hurried back to his own house, Martin thought about what Albrecht had said. Fancy his friend wanting to be a painter! Albrecht's father had certainly sounded very angry.

When he reached home Martin was surprised to find that the big double doors on to the street were still open. He went through the entrance passage into the inner courtyard. Martin's family lived in the upper part of the house. His father's printing works was on the ground floor and noises from the printing room showed that work was not yet over. The head journeyman came out looking hot and tired, and went to wash his neck and hands at the well in the center of the yard.

'It's been a hard day,' he said. 'We've been setting up the new press, and nothing has gone right. Your father will be in a frenzy if Master Koberger comes while it's printing unevenly.'

Martin did not know who Master Koberger was, but he sounded important. It was best to keep out of his father's way if things were going badly, so he ran up the stairs at the side of the courtyard and into the kitchen. Agnes, his big sister, was preparing supper. She often let him taste what she was cooking.

While she got the supper ready, Martin told her about Albrecht. 'I can't understand him. I'd be glad to be a goldsmith,' he said.

'You may be better off as a printer,' said his sister. 'It's a new trade, without lots of rules. In most trades you have to swear an oath of loyalty to Nuremberg every year and you can't leave the city without permission.'

'Why ever not?' asked Martin.

'So that you can't teach Nuremberg skills to outsiders, of course!' said Agnes. 'Now hurry and fetch me some apples. They're packed in straw in the cellar. Supper will soon be ready and Father wants to talk to you.'

A Great Opportunity

In the living room Martin's younger brothers and sisters were already waiting by their places at the dining table. His mother sat by the warm tiled stove, spinning wool and rocking the baby's cradle with her foot. She frowned when she saw Martin come in so late and so untidy. 'What hands, what feet and what a face!' she exclaimed. 'Wash them quickly, your father's coming.'

Martin hurriedly washed at the water cistern by the door, put his damp shoes near the stove, and reached the table just as his father came in.

Martin wanted to ask about Master Koberger, but children were not expected to talk at meals unless their parents spoke to them. Luckily he did not have to wait long.

'Martin,' said his father, 'I think that head of yours has some sense in it, whatever your schoolmaster may say. We have a great chance ahead of us, but I need your help. Anton Koberger, the biggest publisher in Germany, has asked us to do some printing for him. He does such a lot of business that he can't print everything in his own workshop. He doesn't bother with the small jobs that we rely on – pictures of saints and playing cards and pamphlets. He prints books, and sells them all over Europe. If we print his order well, he may ask us to do lots more.'

'What luck!' said Martin. 'What can I do? Can I really help?'

'Yes,' said his father. 'We still need to keep our press for the little pictures going while we are printing Master Koberger's books. We can't afford to give up our usual work. At this time of year we can sell thousands of souvenir pictures of the Holy Relics. But I can't afford to take on new workmen. The new press for books has cost me quite enough already. You must help the journeymen to keep the old press working while I operate the new one. You can start work helping them tomorrow.'

A Simple Idea

Martin had a lot to learn. The next day, his father showed him round the printing workshop. In the foundry Martin watched the type being made. The journeyman typecaster poured hot molten metal into a little mold. When the metal had cooled and hardened he took out the piece of type – a tiny oblong of metal with a raised letter at one end. He made hundreds of these individual letters every day.

'Making each letter separately seems a simple idea,' he said to Martin, 'but until quite recently no one had thought of it! They used to carve the whole page on one block of wood. So they only printed pictures and just a few captions. They didn't bother carving lots of words. It was cheaper to write them by hand!'

In the printing room next door a journeyman was choosing the letters he needed, and placing them, a row at a time, in a long tray. He was copying a handwritten page, which was propped up in front of him. Martin couldn't read the page very well; it was in Latin.

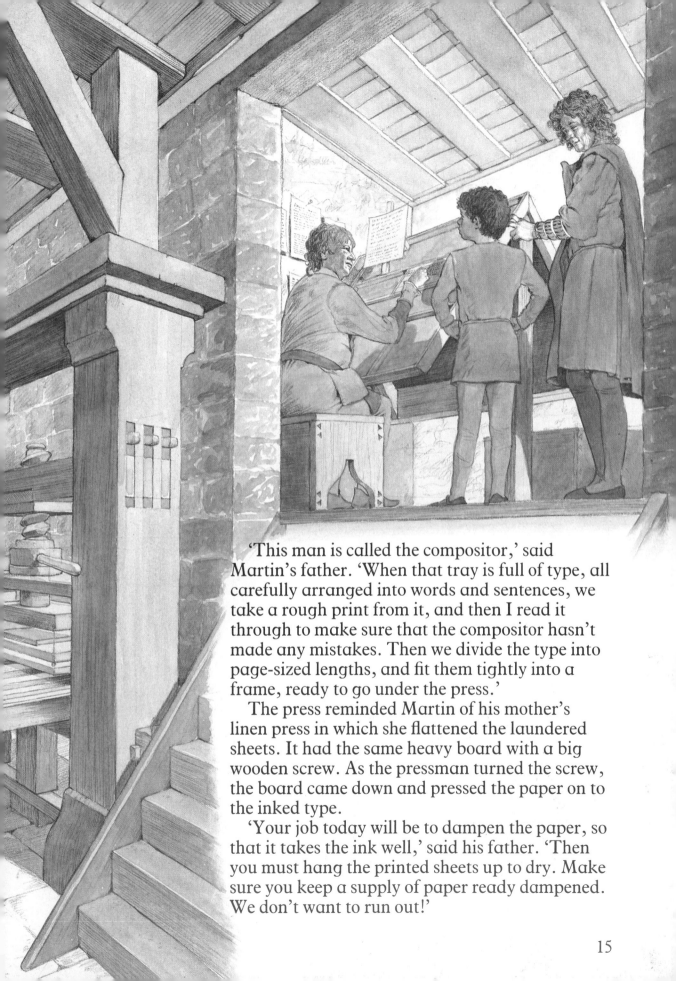

'This man is called the compositor,' said
Martin's father. 'When that tray is full of type, all
carefully arranged into words and sentences, we
take a rough print from it, and then I read it
through to make sure that the compositor hasn't
made any mistakes. Then we divide the type into
page-sized lengths, and fit them tightly into a
frame, ready to go under the press.'

The press reminded Martin of his mother's
linen press in which she flattened the laundered
sheets. It had the same heavy board with a big
wooden screw. As the pressman turned the screw,
the board came down and pressed the paper on to
the inked type.

'Your job today will be to dampen the paper, so
that it takes the ink well,' said his father. 'Then
you must hang the printed sheets up to dry. Make
sure you keep a supply of paper ready dampened.
We don't want to run out!'

15

At the Paper Mill

Martin's next job was to mix ink for the old press that printed the wood-block pictures. The journeyman block-cutter was cutting a new block for this year's souvenir picture. Souvenir pictures were sold to the crowds of people who came each year for the Festival when the Holy Relics were put on public display. The block-cutter drew a picture on the surface of the wooden block and cut away the wood where he did not want it to print. He and the journeyman colorist, who tinted the finished prints by hand, had worked for Martin's grandfather in the old days, when the business printed only playing cards. They were grumpy old men, who didn't like Martin singing as he worked. He was glad when his father asked him to take a message to his uncle at the paper mill.

The mill was just outside the town. Martin smiled to himself as he walked out of the city gate into the countryside. This was better than school!

Martin's uncle owned one of the many watermills on the river. It was very noisy inside the mill. A row of huge hammers was pounding rags into pulp in a long trough. A man was dipping a square frame, with mesh at the bottom, into a wide vat, which stood to one side. When he lifted the frame out, a thin layer of pulp lay on the mesh. This would become paper when it was dry.

'Those hammers are driven by a big waterwheel,' said Martin's uncle. 'Would you like to see it?'

He led Martin outside the mill and down towards the river. Martin could see how the force of the river water, pushing against the paddles on the huge wheel, made it turn.

'Do all these mills make paper?' asked Martin, looking at the other buildings on the river banks.

'No,' said his uncle. 'Water power can do all sorts of work. It can drive wheels to grind corn, for instance. Most important for us here in Nuremberg, it works the big bellows for the furnaces that smelt the metal; and the metal is made into the fine things our town is famous for.'

A Wonderful Offer

Next day, Martin delivered the first batch of
finished work to Master Koberger's printing
house. He was amazed at the number of presses
he saw in the printing room and at the hundreds
of barrels, packed with books, that stood in the
warehouse, waiting to be sent all over Europe.

As he was handing over his parcel, a clerk came
running downstairs. 'Master Koberger wants you
in his office,' he said to Martin.

Feeling very surprised, Martin climbed the
staircase and peered rather timidly round the door
at the top. Two men, leaning over a desk, were
busy talking, and there in the window seat,
listening closely to every word, sat Albrecht!

No one noticed Martin. He took a couple of
steps towards the men. 'That must be Master
Koberger,' he thought, looking at the older man.
'I wonder why he wants to see me?'

The two men continued to talk excitedly.

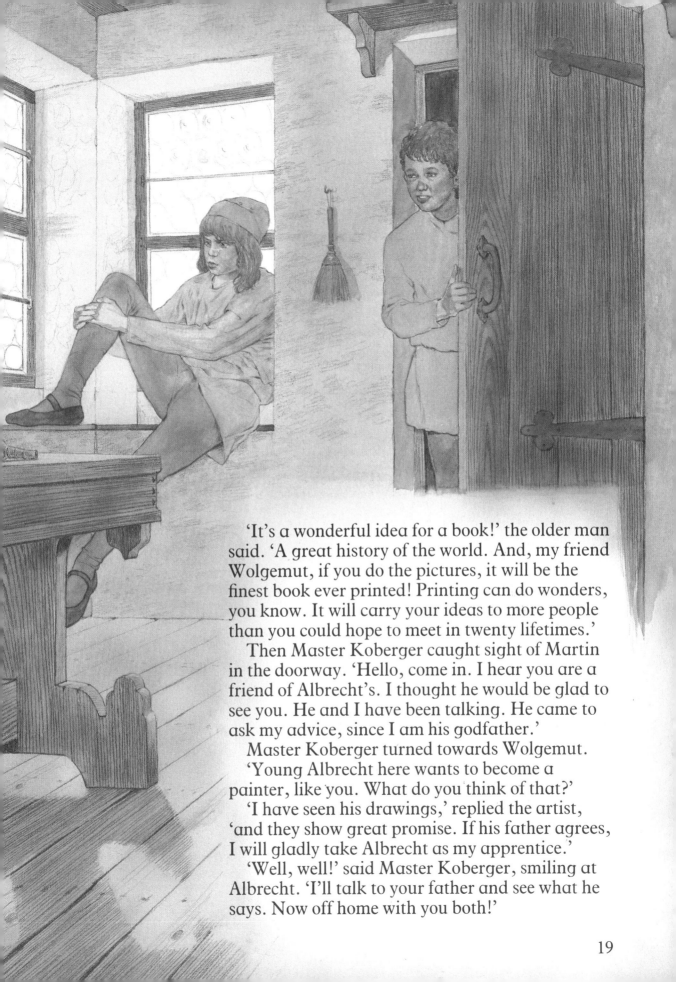

'It's a wonderful idea for a book!' the older man said. 'A great history of the world. And, my friend Wolgemut, if you do the pictures, it will be the finest book ever printed! Printing can do wonders, you know. It will carry your ideas to more people than you could hope to meet in twenty lifetimes.'

Then Master Koberger caught sight of Martin in the doorway. 'Hello, come in. I hear you are a friend of Albrecht's. I thought he would be glad to see you. He and I have been talking. He came to ask my advice, since I am his godfather.'

Master Koberger turned towards Wolgemut. 'Young Albrecht here wants to become a painter, like you. What do you think of that?'

'I have seen his drawings,' replied the artist, 'and they show great promise. If his father agrees, I will gladly take Albrecht as my apprentice.'

'Well, well!' said Master Koberger, smiling at Albrecht. 'I'll talk to your father and see what he says. Now off home with you both!'

A Fight and a Fire

The two boys stopped outside Albrecht's house.

'Would you like to come in?' asked Albrecht. 'If Father is out, I can show you what I'm working on now. Have you got time?'

In the goldsmith's workshop Albrecht showed Martin a design that he was about to engrave on a box. 'It's the case for an astrolabe,' he said.

'Whatever's that?' exclaimed Martin.

'It's a sort of dial that measures the position of the stars,' said Albrecht. 'An astronomer has asked us to make one for him.'

At the back of the workshop a journeyman was polishing a little crown, set with pearls. 'It's a bridal crown,' he said, 'so it must be finished on time, though I'm busy enough as it is, preparing my masterpieces.' Martin knew that these were the test pieces made by each journeyman in order to qualify as a master craftsman. They would be judged by the top craftsman of each guild.

'Look at these,' said the journeyman. 'I've done my very best. Believe me, boys, there's nothing more satisfying than making a splendid object.'

'Yes there is!' said Albrecht excitedly. 'A splendid object can only be seen by a few people, but splendid ideas or splendid drawings can reach thousands, through printing. That's what I would like to do – share my ideas with thousands.'

Martin knew that Albrecht was thinking of what Master Koberger had said, but one of the other apprentices gave a spiteful laugh. 'Share your ideas!' he sneered. 'Nothing ever came out of your head but lanky hair,' and he gave Albrecht's fringe a sharp tug.

Furious, Albrecht seized him by the shoulders and a fight began.

'Watch out!' yelled Martin, but it was too late. A little pot for melting metal, and the brazier beneath it, toppled over. The journeyman quickly stamped out the flames. Only a few scraps of paper on the floor had caught fire, but Albrecht snatched up one in horror. It was the design for the astrolabe. Half of it was burnt away.

The Astronomer

'You'd better clear out of the way for a bit,' said the journeyman. 'I'll tidy up in here.'

Out in the street, the boys looked at one another in dismay.

'If Father finds out about this,' said Albrecht, 'he'll be so cross that he'll never let me go and work for Master Wolgemut.'

'We could ask the astronomer whether he's got another copy of the design,' said Martin.

'I suppose it's worth a try,' said Albrecht. 'But what will he say when he finds out that we've burnt his drawing?'

The astronomer lived in a tall house near the castle. The door was open and servants were carrying in food and drink, as if they were preparing for a feast.

'The master is in his observatory at the top of the house,' said a servant, who thought the boys had come to deliver something.

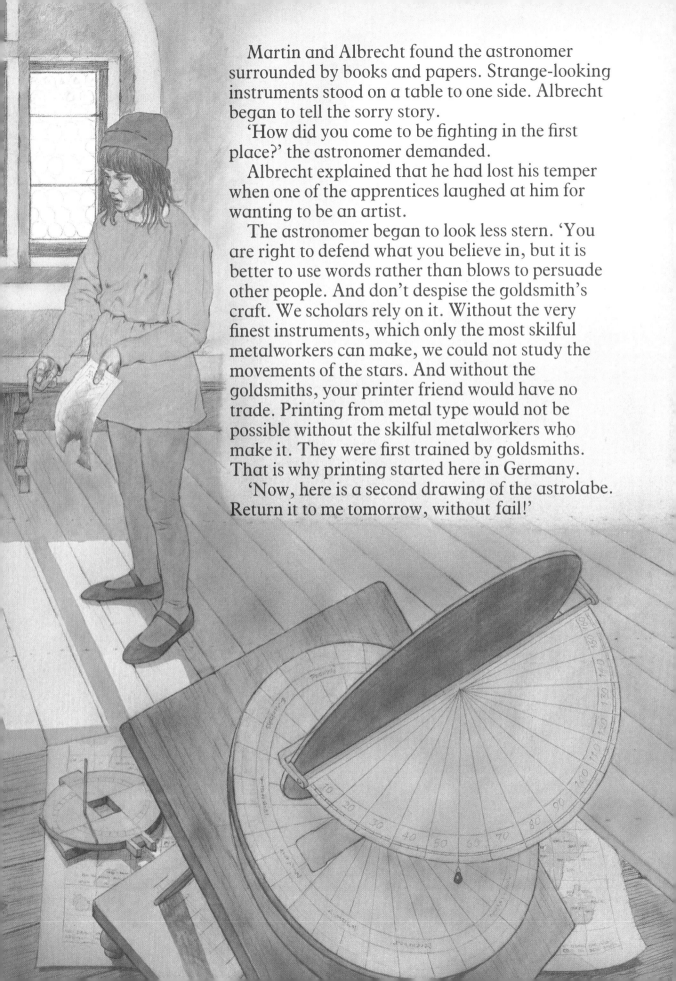

Martin and Albrecht found the astronomer surrounded by books and papers. Strange-looking instruments stood on a table to one side. Albrecht began to tell the sorry story.

'How did you come to be fighting in the first place?' the astronomer demanded.

Albrecht explained that he had lost his temper when one of the apprentices laughed at him for wanting to be an artist.

The astronomer began to look less stern. 'You are right to defend what you believe in, but it is better to use words rather than blows to persuade other people. And don't despise the goldsmith's craft. We scholars rely on it. Without the very finest instruments, which only the most skilful metalworkers can make, we could not study the movements of the stars. And without the goldsmiths, your printer friend would have no trade. Printing from metal type would not be possible without the skilful metalworkers who make it. They were first trained by goldsmiths. That is why printing started here in Germany.

'Now, here is a second drawing of the astrolabe. Return it to me tomorrow, without fail!'

Martin helps his Friend

The next day, as Martin helped the journeymen in the printing workshop, he couldn't help wondering how Albrecht was getting on. Had he managed to copy the replacement drawing of the astrolabe in time? He was glad when his father sent him on an errand to the timber merchant's. It gave him a chance to call in and see Albrecht.

His friend was looking out for him. As soon as Martin came into the goldsmith's workshop, Albrecht pushed the drawing into his hand. 'Father mustn't know,' he whispered. 'I daren't go myself. Please take it back for me.'

Martin did not like to go back to the astronomer's strange house alone but, to help his friend, he agreed. As he approached the house he heard music and laughter.

'You can't come in,' said the doorkeeper. 'Our master is celebrating his daughter's wedding.'

'But I've got something to give him,' said Martin. 'It's urgent!'

Ignoring the doorkeeper's angry shouts, Martin dodged past and ran into the house. Through a doorway he could see the bride, seated with her guests. On her head was the crown Martin had seen in the workshop. The guests were dressed in furs and silk. Martin knew they must be rich merchants, for ordinary people were not allowed to wear such things.

Martin couldn't go into the room and interrupt the wedding feast. What should he do?

With relief, he caught sight of a servant girl. She was carrying wine from the cellar.

'Please, hand your master this,' begged Martin. She took it from him without saying a word. He hardly dared to breathe as he watched her fill the guests' glasses. Then she reached the astronomer's seat. She gave him the paper. He glanced at it in surprise, and then smiled.

Martin breathed a great sigh of relief. He had returned the drawing safely!

The Festival of the Relics

It was Festival Week. This year, Martin had his own print stall in the square. Before the Festival had started, Martin and his father had worked late into the night to print as many souvenir pictures as possible.

Martin looked with satisfaction at his empty stall. He was hoarse from shouting 'Get your souvenir prints here!', but it had been worth it. Every print had been sold. There were so many customers this year! All week, thousands of pilgrims had been pouring into Nuremberg until every inn was full and every spare room let.

'You didn't need my help, after all!' said a voice behind him. 'I see you've sold the lot!' Albrecht had arrived at last.

'I couldn't get through the crowds before,' he said. 'They've put chains across most of the streets into the square, to keep people moving just one way. I had to go right round the outside before I could get across to your stall.'

'I thought you might have been kept in because you were in trouble with your father again,' said Martin, teasing him.

'No,' laughed Albrecht. 'The astronomer was very pleased with my work for the astrolabe. Father is really quite proud of me, though he doesn't show it. I think he will let me be a painter after all.'

Suddenly, trumpets sounded and the crowd became quiet.

'Let's get to the front!' said Albrecht. They squeezed forward, until they were close to the soldiers who guarded the wooden tower from which the Holy Relics were shown. As they watched, city councillors with lighted candles climbed to the top of the tower, followed by priests carrying the Holy Relics themselves. The Bishop of Bamberg raised his hands: 'A blessing on all gathered here, and on this great city and its people. A blessing on you all!'

The great crowd answered, and Martin and Albrecht joined in the loud 'Amen'.

27

Picture Glossary

In the 15th century Nuremberg was a large and prosperous city. Its wealth came from its importance as a trading centre and from the skills of its craftsmen. They made a wide variety of goods – ranging from guns to delicate scientific instruments – and were especially skilled at metalwork. They made many beautiful and extravagant luxury objects for wealthy townspeople to use in their homes.

The metalworker's skills helped develop the technique of printing with moveable type. This invention changed the world by spreading new ideas more widely than before.

Below: Panoramic view of the city of Nuremberg at the time of this story.

Printing with moveable type

A Each letter is individually made in metal, and fixed to a small block of wood. These blocks are then joined up to make words and sentences.

B The letters are made back to front, so that they will appear the right way round when printed (C).

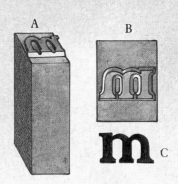

Right : Examples of fine metalwork made in Nuremberg

1 Cup made of agate, a semi-precious stone
2 Gold 'welcome cup'
3 Gilt and silver beaker with a decorated lid
4 Beaker made of ox-horn, with a lid
5 Iron candlestick, shaped like a dragon
6 Mazer (wooden dish) with lid
7 Bronze fountain head
8 Pewter flagon for serving wine

Right: Albrecht grew up to become a famous painter, and lived and worked in this house. He is usually known by his surname (Dürer) today, so the house, which you can visit in Nuremberg, is known as Dürer's House.

Above: Arms and Armor

9 Suit of armor
10 Sword hilt (handle) with bronze decoration
11 Journeyman's hammer for metalworking
12 Throwing axe of forged steel

Right: This map shows Nuremberg's position at the center of trade routes across Europe.

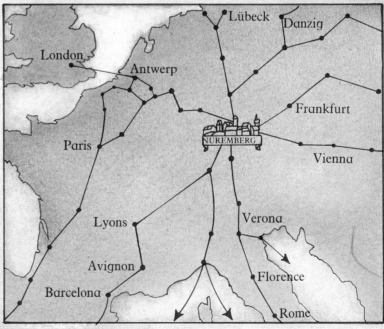